FACEBOOK MARKETING

How to Use Facebook for Effective
Internet Marketing and Social Media Success

KENNETH LEWIS

DEDICATED TO
THE READER

May you be successful in all your business
and entrepreneurial endeavors.

TABLE OF CONTENTS

INTRODUCTION

Facebook is a colossal entity with almost 1 billion daily users interacting with each other and checking their newsfeed for updates about the world. With so many people choosing to access Facebook every day, it is no wonder that it has become one of the greatest marketing assets of this decade.

Facebook actively encourages advertisement efforts on their website and other business relations, providing an abundance of tools and systems for both small and large businesses. However, trying to learn how to market through Facebook poses a steep learning curve. Although a few tips and tricks from tried and tested internet marketing guides are applicable, Facebook needs to be tackled as its own creature, with its own rules.

You need to thoroughly understand how Facebook works on a very fundamental level. This includes topics such as how Facebook determines what content is presented through the newsfeed and the underlying concept of the 'reach' and of organic content.

Your knowledge must also extend to the labyrinthine system of paid advertising and marketing. You need to appreciate the different between a boosted post, a paid advertisement and all the different decisions you should have to make, should you choose to employ either. It is also critical to know how the auction and bidding systems work; the underlying mechanism which determines the cost and charges associated with advertising on Facebook.

This, however, doesn't even cover the tip of the iceberg. You also need to be intimate with the different Facebook business objective goals and the different audiences you can target via all the options Facebook provides. There are the various pricing schemes you can chose, say as pay-per-click, pay-per-impression and optimized pay-per-click that you cannot market without. Additionally, you need to understand the three-part campaign structure of Facebook advertising and the tools offered to manage advertising, such as the power editor.

With these fundamentals covered in the initial chapter, you can then begin to stretch your marketing muscles with Facebook Insights, which presents an entire world of marketing information for you to analyze. If you want to know how many more people liked your content in the past 24 hours, or what your potential reach could be, Facebook Insights is going to be your best friend. Even if you remain mere associates, you need to appreciate Facebook Insights for what the feedback and power it offers you to refine and improve your marketing efforts.

With Facebook Insights now firmly understood, you can start to really bring your marketing tactics to the next level with more advanced strategies. If you are naïve about dark posting or if you think pixels are just to do with your screen resolution, then the strategies within this book will give you an enlightening wake-up call. Learn how to target niche audiences, improve conversions, create custom audiences and re-target missed buyers with the sophisticated and complex opportunities Facebook presents.

With your marketing expertise now reaching intimidating levels, you will then be presented with all the various resources that you can utilize to give yourself the Facebook marketing edge. Find out where you can access Facebook's free 34 part marketing e-learning course, or where you should be waiting to hear the latest Facebook news and updates.

With your Facebook mastery established, you must be prudent to stay on top of the game by keeping up to date with all the changes and updates Facebook is developing for release in the near future. Facebook puts light itself to shame with just how fast it rushes ahead.

If you simply sit on the knowledge of established techniques without taking the initiative to keep your knowledge fresh, then you will soon find yourself a Facebook novice once more. Learn about highly anticipated changes, such as Facebook Reactions, Facebook Immersive ads and Facebook Connectivity - changes that may shake the foundations of the current Facebook marketing platform we know today.

Finally, take your business or product to the next level by learning some of the top SEO strategies in our bonus preview section.

Congratulations on reading. You have already taken the first step to improving your marketing strategy. I trust you will enjoy reading and benefit from the strategies we discuss.

1

FACEBOOK 'ORGANIC' REACH

Originally, all content a user posted on Facebook would be seen by their followers on their news feeds. However, as Facebook became more popular and the average user subscribed to more content, Facebook implemented a system to filter and restrict the amount of content users see. Now, only a portion of content gets seen by followers, which prevents users from feeling overwhelmed as well as protect them viewing from diluted, poor content – or rather content that they simply will not be interested in. This system is called 'Facebook Reach' and refers to how far and how much penetration (i.e reach) your Facebook content achieves.

Facebook reach deals with 'organic' content. Organic refers to content that is naturally filtered through search engine and social media engines. This organic content is then ranked and filtered according to its quality, and thus generates a certain amount of exposure or traffic based on the ranking it receives.

Although most marketers will also employ Facebook Boost and Facebook Paid Advertising, Facebook Reach is where every internet marketer will want to start. If you learn to play the game and abide by the rules, you can still ensure a high amount of your organic content reaches your desired audience. Furthermore, Facebook Reach is free and is a great way for internet marketers to test the shallow waters before they dive in to the deep end.

Facebook Reach uses an algorithm to filter content and decide whether that content is worth your follower's time. The original algorithm, called 'Edgerank' uses three factors (affinity, edge weight and time decay).

Affinity, Weight and Time Decay

Affinity refers to how well two users are known to each other, and how interconnected their lives are. If two users frequently interact across Facebook, frequently tag each other or belong to many of the same groups and share many of the same friends, than these users will have high affinity. Affinity takes into account clicking on user content, liking, commenting, tagging, sharing and friend-ing as measures of connectedness.

It is important to note that affinity is asymmetrical; user A can have a high affinity towards user B without user B having high affinity towards user A.

Additionally, each action you perform on Facebook has a different 'edge weight'. Simply put, certain actions are considered more important and more telling than others. It is easy and non-committal to like or share content. Commenting however, implies a closer relationship between two users. At the very least, it signals more effort. Owing to this, commenting has a higher edge weight than liking and will be more influential in Facebook Edgerank.

Edge weight is believed to be contextual in the sense that certain actions will be weighted higher or lower depending on the users involved, rather than having a static value. If a user prefers to share content, but rarely tends to comment, then sharing content might receive a higher edge rank for this particular user, based upon that particular Facebook habit.

Finally, the Edgerank also considers time decay. Naturally, Facebook desires for their users' newsfeed to stay fresh and current. Therefore, the older content is, the less relevant it is considered. A post that is a day old is designated less important that a post an hour old, which in turn is less important than a 10 minute old post.

It is theorized that time decay takes into account how often a user logs in to Facebook, as well as how often they post. When a user logs in only occasionally, it is redundant to show them posts only from that day – they need to see a range of content from the last time they logged in.

Similarly, if a user posts infrequently, their content might suffer from less time decay than if a user posts several times a day. Naturally, if someone is posting content all the time, the implication is that this content is relatively trivial. Conversely, if someone does not post very often, then they may have something important to say or share.

Edgerank Development

As Facebook grew and gathered more resources to work with, Edgerank became increasingly complex as it continued to factor more and more into the ranking algorithm. Across the internet, many internet marketers still use the term 'Edgerank' to refer to the ranking system of organic content - just be aware that they are unlikely referring to the original system, but whatever algorithm is now in use.

Also be aware that Facebook no longer internally uses the name 'Edgerank' for their newsfeed sorting algorithm. Nonetheless, for the purposes of this book, the ranking system will be referred to as the newsfeed algorithm and any mention of the original system will be made explicitly clear.

Not all the markers and variables that the newsfeed algorithm currently uses are known. Although Facebook often encourages and supports internet marketers using their platform, they also have a vested interest in keeping the workings of algorithms secret.

Essentially, the newsfeed algorithm is intended to produce an accurate and useful ranking, yet internet marketers want to discover how to manipulate the algorithms in order to selectively favor their organic content. The result of this conflict produces an internet arms race; Facebook attempts to refine and develop their newsfeed algorithms faster than internet markers discover and exploit it.

Nonetheless certain factors that the newsfeed considers, which are consistently important, are well known. For example, marketers are increasingly scheduling their organic content to be posted during non-peak hours (evenings and weekends). Naturally, during the working day there tends to be a higher amount of content posted on Facebook by regular users. This influx of content results in more posts being filtered away to keep a user's newsfeed from being overburdened.

For marketers who want to have the greatest reach, it therefore becomes essential to target Facebook 'downtime' where fewer people are posting and it is more likely for your organic content to be seen. Current opinion suggests that the hours between 5PM and 1AM are the most ideal times – ensure that you make the most of Facebook scheduler to hit the inconvenient later hours which you can't devote time to in person.

Additionally, optimized content receives a greater reach than non-optimized content as it receives a greater amount of clicks, likes, shares and comments. How to optimize your content for Facebook is a lengthy topic to address by itself, however the key message can be reduced to a few points. Firstly, keep your posts extremely brief – it is suggested to use no more than 40 characters. If you have a longer message you need to convey, link a source to that content in your Facebook post, rather than just post it.

Secondly, incorporate a high amount of video and images in your content. It is particularly important to use Facebook's native video player rather than popular alternatives such as Youtube. Videos using Facebook's video player are displayed larger then foreign sources, which results in more people clicking and viewing the video.

Thirdly, incorporate 'calls-to-action' using imperative language and asking your users to like, share, follow or perform some activity. Unsurprisingly, if you ask people to do an action, a higher percentage of people actually do it.

Additionally, use hashtags. Hashtags link your content to popular trends, makes your content easier to find and gives you more brand identity.

It is also useful to incorporate or blend well-received topics into your content (emotional or people based stories, animals and children). Of course, this needs to be relevant, but with a little creativity it is easy to achieve, no matter the topic of your business.

Relatability and connectedness with your audience is also crucial to any marketing campaign. Maintaining a personal, authentic 'human' persona behind all marketing efforts is important to stay connected and relevant to your customers.

Facebook Reach Decline

Although organic Facebook Reach still offers a lot of potential for businesses, it is gradually becoming less and less relevant to internet marketers. Overall, organic content is getting harder to push, and is being filtered to a harsher standard. In fact, the decline of Facebook organic reach is so large that many people in the industry refer to the phenomenon as the 'reachpocalypse'.

Certain studies suggest that organic content on Facebook Reach is only seen by 6% of followers – an alarmingly low amount for businesses that struggle to get any sizable amount of followers to begin with.

The reasons for the decline of Facebook Reach are debatable. Marketing critics and internet researchers claim that Facebook has incrementally reduced the relevance of Facebook reach in order to force Facebook marketers already using the platform to shift to paid options. After all, at the end of the day, Facebook is also a business and increased profit is their ultimate goal.

Facebook itself claims that the decline of Facebook reach is due to the massive increase in Facebook content being produced, resulting in increased newsfeed filtering by necessity. Facebook also cites better algorithms for determining high quality content allowing only the choicest posts to be shown on a user's newsfeed.

Regardless of the reason for the decline, all data and trends demonstrate it is indeed real. As a result for the Facebook marketer, it is becoming crucial to be either exceptional at optimizing content or resorting to Facebook Boost and Facebook Paid Advertising to achieve marketing impact.

Facebook Boost

Facebook offers two ways you can pay for their advertising services: Facebook Boost and Facebook advertisement. This section will deal with the first of the two: Facebook Boost.

Facebook Boost is a service that allows you to pay in order to give your organic content more reach. The content you boost appears the same to your followers and shows no signs of being paid for (such as the 'sponsored' label that appears in promoted posts). However, this content will be seen by more of your followers and will appear higher in the newsfeed. Boost is applied individually to each post you wish to make.

To boost a post, you first need to make a business page with Facebook. To do this, you must first login to your regular Facebook account. Then, click the arrow at the top right-hand corner of the screen and select the create page option. After this, choose the business category for your page and start to fill out relevant information for your business page, such as your business phone number. You will also need to upload a profile picture and add your business page to your favorites. Facebook will prompt you to run an ad immediately; however you can choose to skip it for the time being.

Presuming you have done this, the boost button should appear on the bottom left of any business post you make, under the comments section. Clicking the boost button will cause a tab to open with a whole range of decisions you can make regarding your boost. You will be able to select one of three audiences to target with your boost; people who like your page, people who like your page and their friends and people you choose through targeting.

In addition to targeting a specific audience, Facebook also provides you with the means to target specific regions. For most places, Facebook only offers the options to target specific countries, but you can target specific regions and states in the U.S. as well.

You can also target age ranges, gender, and people by interest and hobby. Moreover, you can also define a budget for the boosted post. The budget you choose is a maximum budget and Facebook will never charge you more than the budget you select, although there is the possibility you may be charged less. The greater budget you allocate, the more reach Facebook Boost will give your post.

Budgets can go up to several thousand dollars, but for most small and moderate businesses, smaller boosts of less than $10 can still generate thousands of extra views at a more affordable costs. Boosted posts also allow you to define a duration for the post to be boosted. Posts can be boosted for up to seven days, with a minimum budget necessary per day.

As a general rule of thumb, boosting is most effective for especially important announcements and exceptional content. If you know one of your posts is likely to produce a high amount of engagement relative to your usual posts, then that post may be eligible for boosting.

If you ever choose to use Facebook boost, you will be able to track your boosts performance using Facebook Ads Manager. This will provide you data such as the amount of people who clicked your boosted post, or the amount of people who liked said post. This data is incredibly important in determining whether boosting your posts is worth your money and what return on investment you can anticipate from you efforts. Such topics will be covered later in this book.

Native Advertising

Native advertising is a very popular method of internet marketing where an advert or any other type of marketing content attempts to blend in with the rest of the user's experience. For example, native advertisement tends to be stylized in the exact same way as other content that a web page user is experiencing and it tends to be placed alongside and within the content the user is browsing, as opposed to appearing as its own entity.

The overall effect native advertising creates is that adverts become more 'camouflaged' and more accepted by individuals who see them, as opposed to being ignored or simply not paid attention to. With promoted posts regularly and effortlessly blending into the regular stream of newsfeed content, Facebook is one of the masters of native advertising.

Facebook Promoted Post

Sometimes referred to as Facebook paid advertising, Facebook promoted posts are simply adverts posted onto Facebook. These adverts look very similar to regular posts from other users with just a few minor differences. At the very top left of the advert, the text 'sponsored' will appear – this informs users that see the post that it is indeed an advert.

Similarly, promoted posts can appear not only within the newsfeed but also within the right hand column for desktop users. Otherwise, promoted posts appear exactly the same as regular posts, with perhaps the exception that they often contain different content.

This similarity between the appearance of regular user posts and promoted posts is one of the reasons why Facebook has become such a massive marketing phenomenon.

Promoting a post offers several advantages over making a mere regular post or boosting the reach of your organic content. Firstly, as before mentioned, the Boost feature simply increases your reach amongst your followers and the natural spread of your content across Facebook; promoted posts, however, can access users beyond your possible reach thus enabling you to market to more people. Furthermore, the choices and targeting systems available to a promoted post far exceed that of a boosted post.

To promote a post, first navigate to your adverts manager (click the promote button in the top right-hand corner and select the adverts manager option.

When you first go to the advert manager, Facebook

will take your business through the process of starting a campaign. This may sound rather advanced, but a campaign is simply the structure that Facebook uses to help you organize your adverts and it consists of three parts.

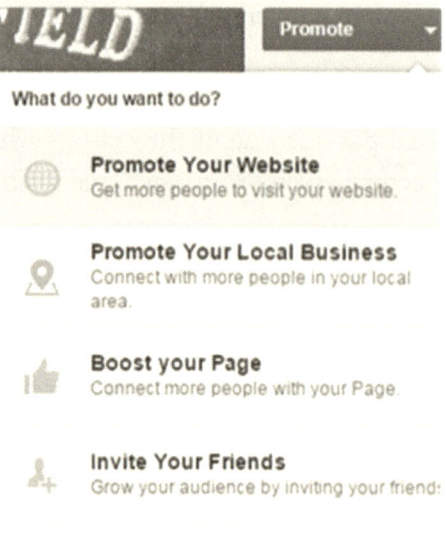

The first part of a campaign is choosing a business objective. The advert manager presents the ten following business goals to choose from:

- Boost your posts
- Promote a website
- Send people to your website
- Increase conversions on your website
- Get installs of your app

- Increase conversions on your website
- Reach people near your businesses
- Raise attendance at your event
- Get people to claim your offer
- Get video reviews

These objects outline the goal you want your adverts to achieve. Using your own marketing knowledge you should be able to determine what business objective is currently best suited to your needs. If you find yourself lost however, Facebook does provide some guidance on what purpose each objective serves, under the 'Advertising Basics' section.

Ad Sets and Facebook Auction

The second part of the campaign structure is 'Ad Sets'. An ad set is simply a collection of different, but associated adverts. All these adverts should promote the success of the original business objective you first selected and be relevant to that particular campaign.

The advantage of ad sets is the control and sophistication that it provides for your advertising efforts. For example, ad sets allow you to run multiple adverts, each displayed to different portions of your targeted audience and then determine the performance of each advert. Using these performance metrics, you can then selectively favor the more popular ads or the ads with better conversion statistics and discard the weaker ads.

Similarly, running an ad set also allows you to display several adverts with a single budget rather then needing to pay a minimum budget per advert (although you will receive the same amount of displays, despite running a greater amount of adverts).

The first process of constructing an ad set is choosing your audience. This process should feel familiar to the boost section on selecting an audience; you will designate location, age range, gender, interests, but also connections, languages, behaviors and some advanced categories to target.

The next stage is determining your budget and the scheduling of your advert, which should also feel familiar to Facebook Boost. You can designate a total budget and budget per day and choose to run ads constantly or on a specific timing schedule.

However, ad sets differ from boost in the methods which you use to determine pricing. Owing to the fact that Facebook receives a greater amount of advertising requests than possible space it offers for advertising via newsfeed, Facebook implements systems to force businesses to compete against one another for the limited advertising spots.

This competitiveness is manifested through an auction scheme to determine the price which a business needs to pay to advertise on their website. Businesses post a maximum bid which they are willing to offer and this bid competes against other businesses with the same goals who are targeting similar demographics.

Where the Facebook auction system differs from a regular auction is how Facebook values adverts differently. In a traditional auction, all buyers are considered the same; only bids determine who wins. Facebook, however, desires to only promote adverts which are deemed high quality and beneficial to their users.

Owing to this, Facebook also considers the adverts attempting to be promoted when they determine what business wins the auction. Higher quality adverts are favored over low quality, to the extent where high quality adverts can win the auction with a lesser maximum bid compared to their peers.

Intrinsic quality is determined by the level of engagement an advert is expected to generate. Adverts which produce high levels of engagement (clicks, likes, shares and feedback) are deemed higher quality and thus garner more competitive prices.

Another aspect of the auction scheme worth noting is

how businesses offer a maximum bid, rather than just a bidding value. Using intrinsic quality as a factor, Facebook will determine how much a business needs to pay to win an auction, relative to the maximum bids of the other buyers. If the maximum bid a business offers is greater than the necessary amount the business needed to win, the business will only be charged the necessary amount.

Facebook will automatically determine what price you should be bidding for and will present this value to you when you construct an ad set, citing this value as the optimized price. However, you can manually go into the auction system and place maximum bids yourself if you wish.

Pricing Systems

To add a layer of complexity, there are actually three different pricing systems. These are as follows:

- Cost per mile (CPM)
- Cost per clicks (CPC)
- Optimized CPM

Cost per mile is how people generally envision paid advertising. By choosing cost per mile, you pay per 1000 impressions. An impression is a just fancy marketing term for a display – you pay a rate to have your advert displayed 1000 times.

Cost per clicks is a slightly more sophisticated option. With cost per clicks you only pay when people click on your advert. Whilst cost per click may seem to be blatantly more advantageous that cost per mile, the drawback is that all types of clicks are considered. This includes people liking and sharing your content, or clicking the hyper link towards your main business page. These engagement actions are obviously beneficial to your overall Facebook marketing efforts, but at the end of the day you end up paying for actions which do not directly lead to profit.

Optimized Cost per click is a relatively recent development in advertising pricing methods. Instead of being charged per click, you are essentially charged per a specific action of your choice. For example, you can pay to be charged when people click towards your website, charged when people like your business page, when people share your content, and many other different factors.

Facebook deliberately ensures that adverts paid for with optimized cost per click are only seen by people who are likely to perform the action you are targeting. For example, if you have optimized for liking, Facebook will try to show your advert to users who like more posts then their peers.

For regular advertisement you will only be offered bid for clicks (cost per clicks) or bid for impressions (cost per mile) as the available options. Bid for clicks is the default option and generally speaking, the best option for most small and medium sized businesses.

Bid for impressions is a much riskier and harder to measure form of advertising, which can lead to large sums of cash being spent without any tangible results products. However, if your overall goal is not to generate conversions or traffic, but just to build brand awareness for some larger reason in your overall marketing plan, then bidding for impressions may be suitable for your purposes.

Optimized cost per click will be available to the larger businesses using the power editor, an advanced advertising system Facebook offers. Optimized cost per click charges more, however it is actually deemed to be less expensive than cost per mile or cost per click. This bizarre logical twist is due to the fact that optimized cost per click schemes produce higher conversion rates then the alternatives.

Therefore, although the baseline expense is greater, as measurement of conversion rates to budget, optimized cost per click is more effective. As a result, if you require a certain increase in conversions for your business, optimized cost per click will require a lower budget. If you are unsure of what pricing scheme is most effective for you, running an ad set with different advertisements using different pricing schemes can help inform you.

Track the cost of each scheme against measurable metrics of their success (i.e conversions), and then determine where you are getting the most bang for your buck. This is called split testing or conversion lift testing and will be covered later in this book.

Advertisement Placement

For large businesses Facebook offers the Power Editor. Power Editor is a free tool designed to help businesses runs vast campaigns with entire clusters of adverts that need to adhere to very specific and detailed sets of information. For most small and medium businesses, the regular advertising campaign should be more than sufficient, but power editor is always available if you want to upscale your efforts.

It is useful to learn about the Power Editor should you be curious about its advantages. As previously mentioned, only businesses using the Power Editor will be offered the optimized cost per click pricing scheme. Yet there is far more to the Power Editor then just this; one of the greatest aspects of the Power Editor is choosing advertisement placement.

There are actually five potential placements for adverts. The first option is within a user's desktop newsfeed alongside all other others. The second option is in a mobile user's newsfeed, and the third option is within mobile-based apps. Content can be optimized for mobile phone users, and Facebook chooses to display mobile newsfeeds slightly differently. Mobile optimization will be covered in later sections.

The fourth and fifth options are to have advertisements appear in the right hand column on a desktop users Facebook display. The fourth option pertains to adds displayed when a user browsers their home page, the fifth when a user browses the newsfeed. These right hand advertisement will be adjacent to the main content on the home page or news feed, but not within it. As a result, these adverts appear less native than the other options, and they may not be visible as a user scrolls down to the lower sections of the web page they are on.

Facebook itself categorizes ad placement in just three ways (Mobile Newsfeed, Desktop Newsfeed and Desktop Right Column), yet internet marketers have pointed out the five-point distinction previously mentioned. Just be aware of the fact that mobile based ads can actually end up in two different places, as can right column adds.

Adverts

The third part of the campaign structure is the adverts themselves. As formerly touched upon, your adverts will appear more or less the same as regular posts. They can contain images, videos, links, content previews, text but also business related content such as offers. The advert manager will provide you with a preview of what each advert will look like on the newsfeed.

Facebook offers detailed suggestions about what adverts are most successful for a business goal on Facebook Guidelines. Although on first glance, most adverts appear identical in structure, aspects such as image size, image ration, text, headline and link description all vary and all have recommended values.

Facebook Advertising Policies

In addition to providing recommended guidelines, Facebook adverts also have a strict set of policies that you must adhere to for your advert to be accepted and remain accepted.

Firstly, Facebook actually enforces the need for images to have a low amount of text within them. An image is not allowed to be covered in more than 20% text, which includes logos. Facebook uses a grid tool in order to determine what proportion of your image is text. You can access the grid tool yourself to check whether you exceed the designate text-image ratio.

Additionally, if you mention Facebook within one of your posts, you must do so in a specific way. Facebook must always be capitalized, and whenever you use a Facebook logo or image, you must use the correct one. Facebook proves brand assets that can be downloaded for free to ensure their business partners are using the correct logos.

Moreover, you must also appreciate Facebook's list of prohibited and restricted content. You are not allowed to promote the sale of any prescription or illegal drugs, tobacco, weapons or adult products and services. You must also not impinge on copyright laws and avoid strong sexual content. Likewise, violent, shocking or gory content are also forbidden.

The before mentioned rules just provide a brief overview of what you might expect from Facebook's policies. For a more thorough reference guide, Facebook makes its Facebook Policies publicly available. As a generalization, most of the policies are rather straight forward and common sense; if you are mindful of sensitive topics and the laws of your region, your adverts should be accepted with little trouble.

2

FACEBOOK INSIGHTS

Facebook Insights is a tool Facebook provides in order to help you track the performance and metrics of your Facebook Business page. Naturally, as a business owner or internet marketer it is essential that you are aware of how effective your Facebook marketing is. Therefore, you need to have an intimate understanding of the unique quirks and eccentricities of the Insights page.

One feature that you will want to dig your teeth into is the export feature. The export button should appear in the top right section of the insights page and it will allow you to download all the data relating to your Facebook page as an excel page or as a .csv file. It is always wise to keep a copy of your data stored in a secondary location, but having an excel or .csv file will make it easier to run third-party software on your data sets if you have specific further analysis in mind.

Before you download this data, Facebook will also give you the choice of whether you want to see 'Page level data' or 'Post level data'. These are what the terms might suggest; page level data information about your Facebook Business page and post level data about information regarding the performance of your Facebook posts.

Finally, Facebook Insights will also allow you to designate a time period to slice your data range from.

Insights Metrics

At the top of the Facebook Insights overview page, you should be presented with three critical metrics relating to your overall performance; 'Total Likes', 'Total Engagement' and 'Total Reach'. All three of these values should also be alongside a small graph and a small arrow indicator with a percentage value, informing you of recent increases or declines of these values.

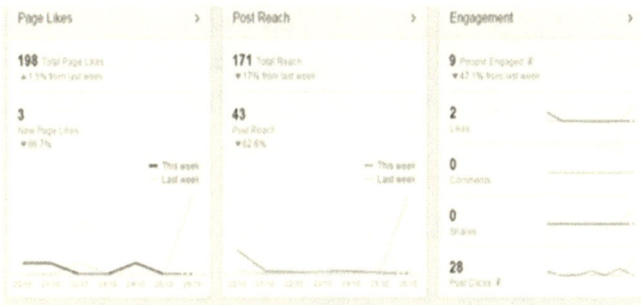

Total likes is self-explanatory and Total engagement tracks engagement activities such as likes, but also comments, shares and post clicks.

Finally, total reach tells you the amount of unique individuals who have seen any content associated with your page within the last week.

The total likes and total reach values are accessible to anyone who visits your Facebook business page. Facebook provides these data so users can have a quick cursory glance at a place and gather the popularity and interest in said page.

Page Insights

The first thing you will see on the Facebook insights section is a table designed to give you a more thorough understanding of the performance of each of your posts, shown in a table. Bear in mind you will need at least 30 fans of your page as well as a few posts in order for Facebook Insights to provide you with any data.

Regarding the table itself, in the first column, the date of each posts will be presented, alongside a provisional title made up from the first few words in that post. The third column will show the type of post and the fourth column will show the reach of each of these posts. The last two columns show the amount of engagement as well as a button to boost a post.

			Reach: Organic/Paid	Post Clicks	Likes, Comments & Shares	
Type	Targeting	Reach		Engagement		Promote
		33		0 2		Boost Post
		111		1 4		Boost Post
		49		2 1		Boost Post
		72		8 2		Boost Post
		113		7 2		Boost Post

Page Insights allows you to perform business-specific content optimization. A few of the more Facebook specific techniques were covered earlier, such as the importance of image based content or using the native Facebook video player.

Nonetheless, all these instructions refer to trends rather then strict rules; it may be the case that text heavy posts, for some peculiar reason, are more effective than image based posts for your business. Above and beyond breaking convention, you may also be able to determine specific patterns about your post content in order to garner what is being received the best by your targeted audience.

Furthermore, Page Insights also allows you to calculate whether your Facebook marketing strategy is being effective. Depending upon your business, you may want to achieve a high reach or alternatively a high engagement with a lower amount of users (or another viable goal).

Pages to Watch

Facebook Insights provides a Pages to Watch section below the Insights it provides on your most recent posts. All marketers keep a watchful eye on their competitors, so Facebook simply formalized the process with the pages to watch section.

This is more than just a mere shortlist of your competitors; it tracks their metrics too. It presents their total page likes, the percentage of increase or decrease from the previous week, the amount of posts they made in the current week, as well as their engagement of the current week. You have to manually add what competitors you wish to track, although Facebook will help by providing relevant suggestions.

As a final parting note on the Pages to Watch, be aware that not all the pages you track need to be viewed as aggressive competitors. It can be mutually beneficial to share, like and contribute to the engagement of similar businesses as this can result to more attention to your business, particularly if you target similar, but distinct audiences. Nonetheless, be wise and don't promote other business over your own, especially when they will be competing for the same customer base.

Insights Sub-Sections

Currently, Facebook Insights is separated into six distinct tabs; an overview section then a breakdown of your likes, reach, visits, posts, videos and people. The previous sections in this chapter have predominantly dealt with the overview section, but there are parts of the other tabs that are well worth highlighting.

The likes, reach and visits tab will present data from the last week (or a calendar section of your choice) in a graphical format. This is useful if you find yourself needing a visual interpretation of your data to summarize overall trends, but these tabs will not provide you with any novel information.

The posts section, however, provides several useful functions. Firstly, it shows you more of your former posts in a format identical to how the overview section presents posts you've made. Unlike the overview section, the post tab will allow you to browse through all the posts you've ever made, rather then just the last five.

Total Page Likes as of Today: 198

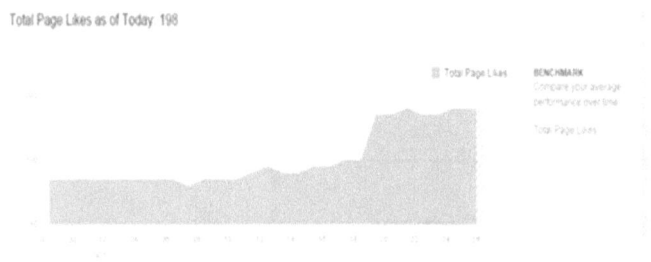

This is more useful for trend observation, but it also gives you the opportunity to present and boost posts that are topical. For example, boosting posts you've made last year about Christmas may once again become relevant during the winter months.

The post section also provides a small breakdown of reach and engagement of your posts by post type (photo, status or link). Additionally there will be a graph demonstrating what time of the day your fans are most active on Facebook. This can obviously help you schedule posts more effectively, but bear in mind that you may have potential fans that do not post during those hours that you have not yet reached.

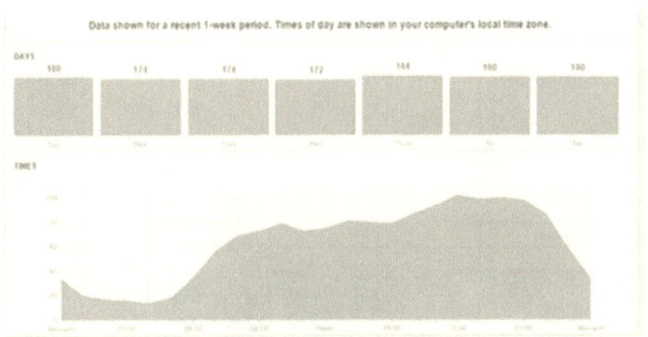

Finally, the post section also allows you to see the top posts from pages that you watch. As always, observe, take inspiration and improve upon the successful formulas your peers are using.

The video section will provide you with three metrics (total views, 30 second views and top videos) about the videos you have posted through Facebook and display this information graphically. If you keep an eye on the performance of your posts in general, you will probably be aware of the performance of video based posts. Nonetheless, if you produce a large amount of video content or appreciate visual representations of data, this section is still useful.

Lastly there is the People tab. This will provide you with a breakdown of where your fans are located, their predominant language, as well as their gender and age range. Use this information to garner whether your audience targeting is both successful, or whether you should actually be capitalizing on audiences that seem to appreciate your current content.

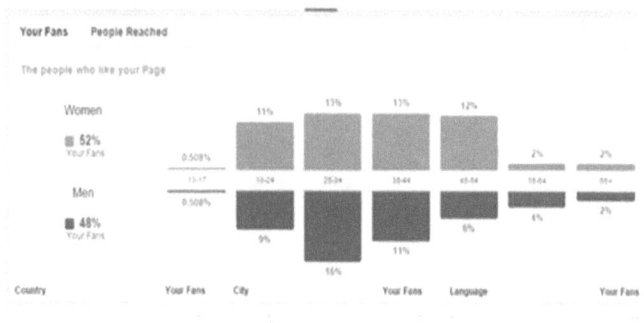

3

ADVANCED FACEBOOK STRATEGIES

Dark Posting

Dark posting is the latest trend that advanced marketers are exploiting. Dark posting involves creating a post, but not releasing it. Then, you create Facebook adverts that encourage users to follow a link to access the unreleased post. The overall result is that dark posts are only accessed by users through Facebook advertising. This bizarre marketing action actually allows you to target customers and test ideas in a very sophisticated way.

The main advantage of dark posting is that you know that users who view the 'dark post' are engaged because they had to traverse through an advertisement to reach the desired post. This allows you to focus on more specific and detailed marketing efforts on very targeted audience that would be wasted on your other audiences.

For example, niche products, by their very nature, will not interest the majority of your audience. If you produce content promoting your niche range on your main wall, then you may lose engagement and confuse followers who are not interested in such niche products. However by creating a dark post, with an advert specifically targeted towards finding people interested in niche products, you can direct niche customers to content they desire without targeting or misdirecting the rest of your potential customers.

Dark posting also ensures that you do not dilute your brand identity. You may wish to push a product or service that runs against your overall brand image, or perhaps you wish to test a new identity, but do not run the risk of spoiling your existing identity if everything goes south. As dark posts are not accessible on your wall, timeline or through the newsfeed, they do not influence your overall image that your users will see.

Facebook Conversion Pixel

The conversion pixel is a tool that Facebook offers websites and applications in order to, unsurprisingly, track conversions. Conversions are meaningful actions people visiting your web page perform. Whenever you receive internet traffic on your website from any source, only a certain percentage of that internet traffic will ever 'convert' to interacting with your website (such as buying a product or registering an account or visiting another page). For most businesses and web pages, conversion rates are around 2%.

Any internet marketer should aim to increase conversions on their website, as a higher rate of conversions lead to higher levels of profit. One of the most effective ways to produce higher conversions is to target individuals with a higher conversion rate, such as individuals who are already planning on purchasing a product and just looking where to purchase it from.

Regardless of your strategy for increasing conversions, you first need to measure them. The conversion pixel can be embedded with your website and then associated with the Facebook ads you produce. Whenever someone goes to your website through a Facebook ad and undergoes a conversion, the conversion pixel will register that action.

The conversion pixel also offers advanced utility; you can alter it to measure only certain types of conversions. This is excellent if you have a particular business goal in mind which you want to measure and increase.

Facebook offers manual guidance for embedding and using conversion pixels under their Facebook Developers Conversion Tracking section.

Facebook Custom Audience Pixel

There are three audiences that Facebook will allow you to target through advertisement: core, custom and look-alike. When you choose statistics such as location, age range or interest, you are in effect designating a 'core' audience; the entire group of people you want to target.

A custom audience refers to an audience you already have data about and are familiar with. Your customer audience for example, may be the people who have subscribed to your website, registered a forum account or who sit on your email list of customers. Your look-alike audience is an audience who appears similar to your custom audience as a demographic, but is not yet engaged or purchasing your service and that you do not have information about.

Depending on what audience you are targeting, your Facebook marketing strategy will be different. Targeting your core audience is great for building brand awareness. Targeting a custom audience is best to encourage existing customers to make repeat purchases or check out your latest deal. Targeting a look-alike audience is fantastic for trying to reach new customers who are likely to be interested in your products but may not have heard of you. When you reach this audience you want to balance brand awareness with more commercial based content.

The fact that Facebook allows you to target custom audiences via advertisements is great if you already have a custom audience prepared. Yet many businesses and start-ups using Facebook as one of their main marketing platforms will be without any custom audiences to worth with.

If you have no custom audiences, the custom audience pixel is a helpful tool to help you create them. The custom audience pixel is similar to the conversion pixel previously mentioned; it is a piece of code you can embed (invisibly) into your website or web pages. Whenever an internet user is browsing these pages, data about their activity is sent towards the Facebook servers to analyze.

Most of this information will be discarded or ignored. However, as an advertiser you can create a set of patterns or actions ("audience rules") that if performed, will instruct the pixel to register. For example, you may wish to track only people who make purchases of $100 or more. If you have the custom audience pixel embedded in your website on your purchasing pages, you can soon produce a list of people who spend this amount. Voila – you now have a custom audience of heavy spenders which you can selectively target for more expensive products.

Facebook guides you through the more complex aspects of custom audience pixel usage under their

Facebook Developers Conversion Tracking section.

Although they are being used at the time of writing, the conversion pixel is considered being removed sometime in late 2016. However, the utility of the conversion pixel (as well as the custom audience pixel) can be found in the Facebook pixel, which is being introduced as a streamlined version of both pixels.

Facebook Retargeting

Retargeting is the internet marketing principle of targeting individuals who have either already purchased, made a conversion, or should be, for some reason, on your radar.

For example, one popular retargeting tactic is to focus on people who almost made a purchase. This may be internet users who traversed your web pages for some time, but left without taking further action. Alternatively, they may people who went through all the motions of spending money, but abandoned your website at the store checkout.

These people are likely to have a great interest in your product or service, but for various reasons decided not to complete the purchase. It may be the case that they decided that they couldn't afford the purchase at that point in time, found another similar product elsewhere or perhaps felt they needed more time to consider.

Retargeting these individuals presents an opportunity for high return on investment advertising. You know these people are invested in your brand or products you just need to convince them to make the plunge. Facebook ensures that these individuals are targeted with adverts on Facebook in order to slyly convince these users to go back to your website and make a purchase.

The way to re-target is to track users who you are intending to re-target and compile a custom audience of these users using the custom audience pixel or Facebook pixel. Then, all you all you have to do is simply post the adverts you have designed to catch these users and drive them back towards your web pages.

Facebook Split Testing

Split testing is a method of determining what adverts or organic content is the most successful. This method involves creating two slightly different posts, with one variable manipulated. It may be the case that you test the same advertising message, but with two different images. Alternatively, you could make an image vs. video manipulation to test whether the effort of producing a video is worth the impact it is generating.

Regardless of the variable and the manipulation you chose, it needs to be singular and controlled. If you change several variables at once, it will be hard to determine what variable, or what combination of variables, are producing any impact. This may be useful if you want quick, easy testing but it will not produce a strong and granular understanding of what posts resonate with your audiences.

Having decided upon the variation you are going to make and the adverts or content you are going to post, you need a method to track them. You can use Google Analytics to embed a custom link that will allow you to recognize the traffic and attention each post is receiving, as well as the data presented on Facebook Insights.

Regardless of what tracking method you choose, post the advert which you anticipate to generate the lowest level of traffic and engagement. Allow this advert to exist for a set amount of time, such as a day or two, then hide the original advert and post the manipulated version.

Allow this advert to exist for the same amount of time, then hide that post too. You can then compare the individual performance of both adverts to determine what manipulation is the most effective. You can even tailor your manipulations with a specific goal in mind, such as increased likes, increased comments, increased clicks and so on.

Facebook Conversion Lift Tests

Conversion lift tests are the method which Facebook advertisers use to systematically and scientifically determine the actual impact of their advertising efforts. Facebook Insights allows you to determine whether you have a certain reach or certain amount of likes, however these results are presented in a way which seems to imply that you are also seeing a return on your investment.

Conversion lift tests allow you to discover whether your adverts are *actually* delivering results. Think of conversion lift testing as the more elegant, smarter brother of split testing. They are both similar, but conversion lift testing just goes the extra mile.

The first stage of a conversion lift test is to create two groups to test within an advertising campaign. One of these groups is a test group — a random selection of

Facebook users who see your adverts. Then you create a control group – a selection of Facebook users who do not see your adverts at all.

After a certain period of time, you provide the conversion data (using the conversion pixel, or a similar tool) of both these groups to Facebook. Using their many algorithms and other mathematical means, Facebook calculates whether the people presented with your advertisement have a conversion, the 'conversion lift'.

If your conversion lift is high, your campaign is having a tangible effect. If it is not, you may want to change your campaign. Go back to split testing and custom audience gathering to determine what sort of campaign will be most effective for your product or business.

4

FACEBOOK RELATED RESOURCES

Facebook itself offers a vast myriad of resources to help businesses and advertisers work with their platform. Nonetheless, between the many tools Facebook offers as well as the various third-party resources, it is easy to get very, very lost. This section aims to briefly outline and direct you to some of the sources of information that can light the way with your Facebook marketing efforts.

Facebook for Business

Facebook for Business is your first stop. This webpage will direct you towards many useful resources, but the content itself it actually relatively simple and introductory. It is mainly aimed at attracting people to use Facebook for business purposes and to choose paid advertising options, but it is worth a browse nonetheless.

Facebook for Business has a Facebook page which is useful for marketing related news and simple tips and examples. It also provides an entire range of marketing video tutorials for you to browse at your leisure.

Facebook Help Center

Facebook outlines the purpose of all their tools and systems within the Facebook Help Center, although sometimes it can lack the down to earth and 'in between the lines' meaning that an objective commentators can impart. However, it does provide a large amount of depth and it will link you towards other relevant topics.

The help center has a specific sub-section called the advertiser help center which not only describes and links the advertising related topics, but holds your hand through the entire process of discovering, considering and implementing advertising on Facebook.

Facebook Business Manager

Facebook Business Manager is a resource aimed at larger companies that are managing several Facebook pages at once and have, or aim to have, wide systems of advertising and content production.

This is the type of resource you may consider using if you have several people working on your Facebook efforts and need to control and delegate tasks efficiently. Facebook Business Manager offers several privacy based features, such as circumnavigating the need for colleagues to be Facebook friends (a potential issue if work/personal boundaries arise). It also offers several levels of password control to prevent employees working within the same company from accessing all levels of the company's advertising campaign.

Facebook Studio

Facebook Studio is a Facebook based website which aims to showcase and celebrate successful Facebook campaigns. Every year Facebook Studio presents awards to the campaigns which have been the most influential and have had the greatest impact – those campaigns that have gone viral. Their content can then be sampled in an interactive gallery. This is a fantastic place to brush up your advertising skills and learn from the masters.

Facebook Newsroom

Facebook Newsroom is Facebook's official page for

Facebook related news and press releases. Facebook is always changing and the Facebook of tomorrow will be different from the Facebook of today. It was only two or three years ago that organic content was king, and the original Facebook Edgerank formula was still influential. Yet nowadays it is all about paid advertising, re-targeting and conversions.

How Facebook operates in a few years time is yet to be determined – but it is still wise to listen to the words of those that are currently steering the ship. Simply put, if you do not keep up with the pace, you will lose out. Even above and beyond the direct marketing related changes, keeping a vested interest in Facebook's position and initiatives as a company is guaranteed to be a sensible move.

If you are investing large amounts of time and resources in to creating your Facebook marketing efforts, it is obviously wise to stay current on anything that might improve or destabilize Facebook as a platform. Facebook releases the financial results of their business every quarter. Take an interest and stay up to date with how Facebook is performing.

Furthermore, Facebook related initiatives may be a great way to give your content an organic boost. For example, one of Facebook's most recent projects, TechPrep, which was announced via Newsroom, aims to help under-represented groups develop and train in computer science related skills. This may present an opportunity for IT related businesses to market their products and services.

Facebook Developers

Facebook Developers is the body of Facebook that is working on many of Facebook's auxiliary technologies and software. In particular, Facebook Developers works on the development of Facebook associated applications and plug-ins. If you want to stay current with the technological aspects of Facebook - particularly app features - then keeping up to date with Facebook Developers is key. Facebook Developers also provides a wealth of information regarding how to monetize and market app-based projects.

Likewise, you will want to stay up to date with the Facebook Developers page on Facebook itself, which will post relevant development news.

Facebook Blueprint

Facebook blueprint is a service Facebook provides in order to teach people how to use Facebook for business purposes. It is a structured, 34 part 'e-learning' course with video tutorials aimed to take you through every aspect of Facebook marketing. It is also entirely free and is well worth the effort to check out.

TechCrunch

Although Facebook is obviously a great source of information about itself, you will still need to frequent third-party sites. Naturally, Facebook as an organization will only ever present to you a biased, Facebook friendly perspective on all the news, tools and services they provide. You will never receive outright lies or even genuine mistruth from Facebook, but an outsider perspective is still useful for keeping a balanced viewpoint.

TechCrunch is a web-based organization that follows and covers a diverse range of internet based companies and technological developments, including Facebook. Here you can read TechCrunch Facebook articles which will give you a digestible, but nonetheless in depth review of recent Facebook activity.

Adroll

Adroll is a massive internet based advertising agency that encompasses many platforms. Adroll does advertise in association with Facebook, but also with most of the large internet agencies such as Twitter and Google. Adroll specifically focuses on re-targeting and ensuring that potential customers with high conversion rates find their way back to your website or web page.

Adroll is particularly useful for building and generating data sets for custom audiences and aims to service both small and large business partners. Adroll is a paid service, so consider whether they are right for you.

5

STAYING UP TO DATE:
CURRENT DEVELOPMENTS

In the previous chapter under the newsroom section, we discussed the overwhelming imperative to stay in touch with all the changes and updates Facebook is making. This chapter aims to stay true to that message by walking you through some of the major updates and changes that Facebook itself has made in the past year, and its plans for the future.

Mobile, Mobile, Mobile!

Although it has been mentioned several times throughout this book, it is essential to re-iterate that mobile usage is extremely prevalent and impactful for Facebook. In 2014, it was revealed that 78% of daily U.S users were accessing Facebook through their mobile. This number is even bigger in 2015, with 844 million of the 968 million daily active users being mobile-based (87%). If you are marketing through Facebook, you are marketing through mobiles, period.

Therefore, you don't just need to consider mobile phone content optimization, you must *prioritize* it. There are a few points that must be clearly understood here. Firstly, the Facebook mobile app only presents a newsfeed, and none of the other auxiliary features - such as the right hand column on a desktop. Your advertisements and content must be presentable on mobile devices, or you are simply missing the overwhelming majority of Facebook users.

Secondly, visual effectiveness and parsimony is far more important on mobiles compared to on a desktop. The text that appears readable through your P.C will appear minuscule on a mobile device. Text needs to be kept to an absolute minimum, but where it is used, it should be large. Otherwise, the same principles that produce good content on a desktop still apply to Facebook mobile marketing targeting.

Facebook Reactions

Facebook is in the process of experimenting with changes to the like button and liking system. Currently, the liking system is rather binary; you either like a post or you do not. There is no middle ground or way to signal that you dislike a post. In order to rectify this, Facebook is experimenting with a seven button system that not only has a like button, but also a 'love' button as well five emoji (small stylized faces), which have been termed 'haha', 'yay', 'wow', 'sad' and 'angry'. This system is called Facebook Reactions, and at the time of writing is being tested with Facebook users in Ireland and Spain.

It is not yet clear how to interpret Facebook Reactions in the scope of internet marketing. One anticipated impact is that marketers will have more information to work with, but a harder time actually determining meaning. The reactions system is designed to be easy to use and increase the amount of quick fast-paced interactions users make in Facebook. Therefore, it is probable that marketers will be able to receive and track a greater level of engagement via the reaction system.

However, determining what the Facebook user is actually *signifying* by the emoji may be rather obtuse. The simplicity of the liking system allows marketers to easily gain a picture of how well their content is being received – simply track the likes. Yet it is not clear how certain emoji should be understood at all.

'Wow' could suggest awe and a positive effect, but it could also be interpreted in the sense of being amazed at the audacity, rudeness or inappropriateness of a certain post. This could pose obvious problems for marketers who receive high amounts of ambiguous emoji, or emoji used in contextual ways. For example, it also is not unusual for modern forum goers to post a happy face in a sarcastic or passive-aggressive way.

Nonetheless, as it currently stands the emoji system is also intended to help users express an array of positive emotions. Although 'sad' and 'angry' are included in the reactions, they are outnumbered by the outright positive reactions 'like', 'love', 'haha' and 'yay'. Facebook theorizes that by increasing the level of positive emotions their system can express, they will increase overall activity (based on the principle that when people feel positive, they are more inclined to engage).

From a marketing perspective, what you should anticipate are changes to the organic newsfeed algorithm to favor posts with high levels of positive reactions, as well as potentially penalize 'angry' reactions. If the reaction system does eventually reach the live Facebook, these algorithms are bound to be newsworthy – so keep an eye out. Similarly, it is also likely that these algorithms are going to be refined and updated, so stay current to the metaphorical ground and listen for any changes.

Global Connectivity and Internet Connection

Facebook already has a massive user base in western, developed regions. However, it is rapidly expanding into the developing world, and to use Facebook's own words, the platform is making changes to 'make sure another billion people can connect using Facebook'.

What this actually entails is that Facebook is making changes to the newsfeed to also take in to account internet connection speed and quality. Developing markets are less likely to have fast or stable internet, and therefore Facebook is planning to accommodate poor internet connection into their newsfeed algorithm.

For example, image based content and video based content - the reigning king and queen of Facebook content - often fail to load when an internet connection is weak. As a result, poorly connected users are marginalized as they cannot see the majority of content posted.

In order to help video and image content, anticipated changes include a focus on loading the currently viewed story first, instead of loading an entire newsfeed at once. Similarly, Facebook is also developing systems that will allow lower quality photos and images to be presented to poorly connected users, as opposed to nothing at all.

Facebook will also take a step backwards and filter less image and video based content into the newsfeed for users with poor connections. This could have massive implications for mobile based users whose connections tend to be more precarious and reliable than desktop users, especially when they are not at home.

Finally, Facebook is also working on systems to present older stories and content to people who cannot load an updated newsfeed. In terms of Facebook marketing, connectivity based changes may present the possibility of introducing a shift away from image or video based content. It is unlikely that these mediums will disappear entirely or become irrelevant, but their popularity may decline.

This will be particularly relevant for marketers whose product or service has an international/developing world audience. At the very least, it is worth being aware that you will need to understand how internet connection affects upload speeds and how this will affect your target audience.

Immersive Ads and Instant Articles

Facebook doesn't want to share the internet with anyone else. Although Facebook is obviously interested in reaping the rewards of businesses advertising through their website, the notion of actually directing their internet traffic to other web pages is actually disadvantageous for them. Simply put, Facebook wants you to stay on Facebook - because that is good for Facebook.

To solve the dissonance between the desire to host advertising and the imperative to keep users on Facebook itself, Facebook is developing immersive ads which was announced in September, 2015. Immersive ads are advertisements that load within Facebook, rather than opening a new tab or browser and loading separately.

This is mainly a mobile-related issue; mobile phone internet-browsers load so slowly that many people abandon the prospect of watching adverts they are interested in due to loading times. By having immersive ads, in platform, adverts can load much quicker for mobile users for the mutual benefit of Facebook and the advertiser.

There is, in essence, the same change for text and multi-media based articles being developed simultaneously called 'Instant Articles'. This will allow you to load lengthier articles and entire galleries of images or videos within a newsfeed, instead of through another website or Facebook profile.

The extent of immersive ads and instant article development is so profound that Facebook is providing 'buy' buttons on these adverts, which will allow purchases through Facebook without even having to access the advertiser's website.

From a marketer's perspective, this will enable a greater range of the types of advertisements that can be presented through the mobile. It will certainly force advertisers to reflect and dedicate more effort to mobile based advertisements. Regardless of how these changes influence marketing, there is little doubt that they will, so be prepared and keep sight of them on the horizon.

Video Actions

In July 2015, Facebook updated their newsfeed algorithm to give more weight to certain actions associated with videos. Facebook theorized that certain actions, even if they do not lead to engagement such as likes, still signal a certain amount of interest to the video. For example, watching a video more than halfway through or expanding the video window to full screen indicates that those videos are meaningful, even if this isn't being conveyed through engagement actions.

As a result of this change, users who display higher levels of meaningful video actions will receive both a higher proportion of video based content, and this video based content will also be presented earlier in the newsfeed.

As video content was already hugely popular, this algorithm provided little change to the actual amount of video content produced or its overall significance. However, it does pave the route for Facebook to provide more video action based metrics for marketers to consider and analyze in the future.

Hoax Update

In January 2015 Facebook updated the newsfeed algorithm to better filter and flag 'hoax posts' in the newsfeed. Hoaxes are essentially classified as spam; they are either posts that attempt to scam users or they deliberately misrepresent information and exaggerate news in order to generate internet traffic and engagement with the hoax website.

Facebook already provided a system to flag certain posts for a myriad of reasons, such as if they are overly sexual, offensive or contain excessive amounts of violence. However, with the hoax update, Facebook now gives users the option to flag posts as 'false'. Posts repeatedly flagged as false will be signaled that they have been flagged to users who see them. If a post reaches a certain number of times as being flagged as false, it will simply be removed from the newsfeed altogether.

The overall effect of this update is a forceful push into higher quality advertising content. Facebook already encourages advertisers and content producers to deliver content that is of a certain standard, yet now poorer quality posts are being penalized even more so than previously.

From a marketing perspective, if you ensure your posts are high-quality and provide value then you have nothing to worry about. However, if your business model relied upon traffic from these low-quality posts, then it is best to reconsider how you wish to go about your Facebook marketing campaign.

Facebook Profile Development

Facebook is developing ways to improve the profiles of users, especially users interacting with Facebook from their mobile. Currently, Facebook is beta-testing incorporating looping video clips into Facebook profiles, instead of just a mere profile picture.

Similarly, Facebook is encouraging profile picture and banners that flicker between multiple images, as opposed to one static image. This is due to Facebook's philosophy that profile pictures display someone as they transition and move through life - so the profile picture should also be dynamic and demonstrate change.

As an internet marketer this may present greater opportunity for brand identity and image management. A looping video clip, even if only short, allows you to display more personality and individuality than a static photo ever could. Similarly, flickering photos give you the ability to convey a greater sense of the intended atmosphere or message then a singular photo.

Ads Manager App

For some businesses and individuals, Facebook marketing is a full time job. At the very least, it is important to be able to access and control advertisements through a multitude of mediums, including mobile phones. Fortunately for these very individuals, Facebook released the Ads Manage App in February 2015. This feature allows you to control your adverts through your mobile.

The manager app doesn't give you the full control and power that your desktop based Facebook activities will provide, but it nonetheless offers several useful services for your advertising efforts. You are able to keep track of an adverts performance, edit ads that you have already made, organize budgets and schedules and create new ads through the ads manager app.

CONCLUSION

Congratulations again on taking the time to read this book and sharpen your online marketing knowledge – you have already taken the first step to increasing the success of your business.

I trust this book was able to help you gain the tools to truly master Facebook marketing. For any business in the modern era, this social media platform presents an opportunity with so much potential that it would be an egregious mistake to ignore it.

This guide has taken you through the process of becoming an expert in Facebook marketing. We began by gaining a ground on the basics of Facebook marketing; the difference between organic content and inorganic content, the concept of Facebook reach, the structure of a campaign advertising system and other foundations.

We investigated Facebook Insights; we advised how you may want to interpret the data this feature offers and what particulars you should focus on in this domain.

KENNETH LEWIS

We explored advanced Facebook strategies. We discussed how to create enigmatic 'dark posts' as well as how to use pixels to measure conversions and create custom audiences. Additionally, we described methods on how to re-target potential customers as well as how to intelligently and logically test and manipulate advertising performance via split testing and conversion lift testing.

We supplemented your Facebook credentials with a range of Facebook related resources for you to investigate and refer back to whenever necessary. If you wish to study further, you now know how to work with services like Facebook Blueprint or Facebook Studios as source materials.

Finally, the last chapter brought you back down to earth. You were reminded that your Facebook marketing knowledge is only useful if it is current and fresh. To help keep you up to date, we provided you with important developments and projects Facebook has unveiled in the last year. You now know the importance of staying abreast of any impactful changes, such as Facebook Reactions, but also subtler fine-grained changes to the newsfeed reaction, such as hoax updates.

The next step is to go to your Facebook page and apply the lessons you have learned here in the real world. Re-think your internet marketing strategy.

How can the most powerful social media marketing tool be used to bring you product or business to the level? We have explored the topic to an utmost depth here – the tenacious action you now take will be your next teacher.

I wish you the best of luck; may you go viral and prosper!

SHARE YOUR EXPERIENCE

Finally, if you enjoyed or benefited from this book, then I would like to ask you for a favor:

Would you be kind enough to leave a review for this book on Amazon?

It would be greatly appreciated!

Visit Amazon.com and search 'Facebook Kenneth Lewis' to be brought to the book's page in which you can leave your feedback.

Thank you, and best of luck on bringing your business to the next level.

BONUS EXCERPT

SEO 2016:
A Complete Guide to
Search Engine Optimization

Search engine optimization (SEO) is the internet art of making a particular website or webpage appear higher on the results of a search engine list. Almost every internet user in the 21st century finds the majority of content they wish to view through websites such as Google or Yahoo. Whether people are looking for an answer to some pointless trivia they don't know or whether people are actively looking for products to buy, search engines are the tool for the job.

However, it is not enough for a website or webpage to be listed on a popular search engine like Google. If a website isn't located on the first page of results, or even the first two or three entries, chances are the majority of searchers are not going to look at that webpage.

If people are not looking at a particular webpage then the purpose of that webpage, such as advertising or product sales, will not be fulfilled. Ultimately, getting a webpage to appear as the first, second or third result on a popular search engine results in a massive difference in the amount of internet traffic they receive and corresponding purchases.

With this in mind, any business that uses the internet to attract customers or sell products *needs* to be familiar with search engine optimization. Search engine optimization is simply too vital to ignore.

Yet search engine optimization is far from easy. It is a multi-faceted, complicated concept that requires intelligent manipulation and research of several corners of the internet.

To master SEO, you need to produce quality content or other attractive goods to generate initial interest. You also need to systematically and continuously increase the amount of links and references to this content via blogs, social media and other sympathetic websites.

It is also of utmost importance to know your audience and consumer better then you know yourself. If someone is looking to find a product or service online, you need to be intimately familiar with what words or phrases that person will enter in the search bar. It is of no use being the highest result for a search entry that no-one is entering. Researching and understanding what keywords people use when looking for your product or market area will increase the likelihood of people finding your content.
You also need to learn how to tactfully and skillfully

embed these keywords in your website or webpage content in intelligent ways, resulting in a greater chance that a search engine will match search entries to your webpage. Conversely, introducing irrelevant or misguided keywords in your text will confuse and bewilder the search engines, attracting the wrong consumers and audiences to your page. Moreover, simply spamming keywords within your text will reduce the quality of content, lowering your audience retention.

All these before mentioned factors barely scratch the surface of search engine optimization. Learning how to exploit social media for your own ends is another crucial skill; you need to be effective and efficient in getting social media users to share and forward the content you produce for free advertising and greater connectivity.

To further pile on the complexity, your website or webpage needs to be attractive and original in design. Global companies such as Apple and Samsung have mastered simple, zen-inspired layouts that retain the attention of internet goers through carefully crafted aesthetics.

Even more importantly, search engines use a variety of markers, calculations and numerous other factors in their algorithms to determine which website finishes first in the SEO race. Understanding the official and formal purposes of meta-tags, headers, spiders robots, paragraphs and cannon descriptions in your website page HTML will give you the insight to convince the search engines you are the best result they can find.

Another factor to take in to consideration are third-party websites and auxiliary resources. These tools can provide you with data and statistics to make all the previously mentioned SEO techniques more accurate and informed. They will provide you will a wealth of useful information such as the exact level of user retention for your website or the conversion rate from website views to product purchases. All of these numbers and charts can help you distill and refine your SEO practices until your techniques are well-polished and your SEO success is inevitable.

Finally, you need to be aware, at least to some extent, of what *not to do*. The more you learn about SEO techniques and the greater level of insight you gain, the greater the temptation can be to shortcut the system; to attempt to cheat and abuse the tendencies of the search engines for your own gain.

Let it be made clear; there is nothing saintly or innocent about SEO; all SEO techniques and attempts are for the purpose of profit or some other marketing feature. Nonetheless, certain techniques and certain actions are considered unfair or especially exploitative and will not be tolerated by the search engines you rely upon. Search engines are becoming smarter and the methods they use to find websites are increasingly refined.

If a search engine recognizes that you are using a lazy or dishonest measure to increase your SEO, it may deliberately ignore that content or punish your website by placing it further down the search engine results. If you go too far, your website or ISP can be blacklisted, ensuring that it will not appear on a search engine again. To avoid these sorts of results requires understanding what lines not to cross and the insidious techniques that lead you into dangerous waters.

All of this required learning may seem overwhelming at initial glance. Fortunately, this book will break down all these techniques into bite-size digestive instruction and tips. After reading *SEO 2016* you will learn everything you need to know to improve your internet presence and business' success through wise and effective SEO management.

To access the rest of 'SEO 2016', visit <u>Amazon.com</u> *and search 'SEO Kenneth Lewis'. Alternatively, you can also listen to the audio format of this book by visiting* <u>Audible.com</u> *and search under the same keywords.*

OTHER WORKS BY KENNETH LEWIS

A Beginner's Guide to Internet Marketing: 17 Proven Online Marketing Strategies to Make Money Online

Facebook Marketing: The 25 Best Strategies on Using Facebook for Advertising, Business and Making Money Online

Passive Income: Make Money Online and Achieve Financial Freedom – How to Make $500 - $12K with Only $50

Social Media Domination: Social Media Marketing Strategies with Facebook, Twitter, YouTube, Instagram and LinkedIn

Procrastination: 7 Simple Strategies to Overcome Procrastination, Increase Productivity and Develop Time Management Strategies for Life

Interview and Get Any Job You Want: Employment Techniques and How to Answer Toughest Interview Questions

All books are available in e-book format, and many are also available in audio-book and paperback format as well. Visit Amazon.com to view available editions.

ABOUT THE AUTHOR

For over thirty years Kenneth has been active in the business and marketing force, working for various companies as well as pursuing his own independent projects. He has most recently begun publishing introductory books on internet marketing and other various aspects of social media as a way to share his passion and interests with those who are new to these domains.

His books aim to be practical, easy to understand and follow. His books also serve as reference guides to those who are already somewhat familiar with the online marketing sector.

In his spare time, Kenneth enjoys golfing, fishing, and spending time with his family at their lake house. Kenneth is also an avid cook and enjoys experimenting with different recipes.